Bringing Forth Justice

Basics for Just Christians

ARCHBISHOP DANIEL E. PILARCZYK

PAULIST PRESS
New York • Mahwah, N.J.

Cover design by Moe Berman.

Library of Congress Cataloging-in-Publication Data

Pilarczyk, Daniel E.
    Bringing forth justice : basics for just Christians / Daniel E. Pilarczyk.
      p. cm.
    Includes bibliographical references.
    ISBN 0-8091-3690-2 (alk. paper)
    1. Christianity and justice—Catholic Church. 2. Catholic Church—Doctrines. I. Title.
    BX1795.J87P55 1997
    261.8′08′822—dc20   96-35131
                                                          CIP

Published by Paulist Press
997 Macarthur Boulevard
Mahwah, New Jersey 07430

Printed and bound in the
United States of America

Contents

Introduction

We all seek justice. The four-year-old who screams out, "It's not fair," is calling for justice. At work, at school, even in games, we expect equal and predictable treatment for everybody. It's only just that things should be that way. If we have been wronged in a business transaction, we can go to court to get things rectified, to get justice for ourselves. Almost instinctively, we feel that someone who has committed murder or theft should be punished. Justice must be done.

Even as we all want justice to be done, so also we know that we are all called to practice justice, to act justly to others. We know we are expected to pay our just share of taxes. If we are an employer, we know we are expected to treat our employees justly. Even the most nonpolitical of us knows that we all bear a common responsibility for seeing that the civil society in which we live enacts just laws and administers the laws that exist in a just way. We know we are all called to practice justice because we all share the common enterprise of human life, and human life cannot flourish without justice.

The classical definition of justice is "the strong and firm will to give to each what is his or her due." Justice is concerned with rights and duties, with receiving and owing, with claims and obligations. It means seeing that I get what's coming to me and that others get what's coming to them. It is involved with maintaining balance and fairness between people in many different contexts. It is the virtue that is concerned with rightness in relationships.

But knowing that, there is still a lot more to know about justice. Who decides what is due to each? On what basis is that determination made? What are my rights as a human being, as a member of society, as an individual relating to other individuals? Where do these rights come from? How do I know if I am being just to others and if others are being just to me? What is the role of government and law in all this?

Questions about justice tend to be complicated. When I was a seminarian, the common opinion among seminarians was that the chapters on justice in the moral theology books were the most difficult of all. There always seemed to be another aspect to be taken into account, another principle that had to be balanced off with the principle that seemed to be the primary one. Moreover, the field of justice ranges from the simplest interpersonal transaction to the rights of workers to organize to the morality of atomic weapons. Almost every aspect of human life has a dimension of justice to it, and human life is complicated.

We have a whole body of specific teaching about justice, particularly its economic and political dimensions, in the writings of popes from Leo XIII to John Paul II. It is important teaching, but it's complex and all of it is written in a necessarily ponderous style that most people find hard to read and digest. It's not that the popes were trying to make things difficult. The subject matter itself is difficult.

Yet even with all this, we don't seem to have all the answers. When it comes to dealing with specific questions of rights and justice, there is often difference of opinion between people of learning and goodwill.

But even if the professional study of justice is demanding in general, and the sources in which the Church's specific teaching is found are heavy, and not all the answers are definitive and clear, that doesn't absolve ordinary Christians from trying to come to grips with justice. After all, the practice of justice is not reserved to people with graduate degrees in theology. It's supposed to be part of the life of every follower of the Lord. Every Christian is supposed to be a just Christian.

Because justice is so important in our human existence, we need to be clear about what justice is and where it comes from. We need to understand that it is not a series of humanly established conventions that are binding on everybody because everybody has agreed to them but rather a natural consequence of what God has created us to be. We also need to be aware that there is more than one kind of justice, that the justice that governs a purchase in a drug store, for example, is not the same kind of justice that governs the relationship between civil government and the taxpayer. Because justice is a matter of rights and responsibilities, we need to understand what is involved in rights and how rights relate to responsibilities. We need to understand the relationship between justice and charity. We need to have some idea about how each of us is called to pursue justice in the various contexts that make up our human existence. We need to be clear about these matters because justice is too important to be played by ear.

That is why I have decided to write this book: to teach about justice so that people will know how to be just. In the chapters that follow, I will try to explain where justice comes from—how our rights as human beings are rooted in what God made us and the world to be. I will have something to say about the relationship between rights and responsibility and about the various contexts and ways in which justice is to be lived out. This will not be a scholarly dissertation; rather, it will be an attempt to help ordinary people understand what justice means for them and for those with whom they share God's world. What I offer is not my personal opinion but the traditional teaching of God's Church based on God's Word in Scripture and on the reflection of God's people over the centuries.

But there is still another side to justice. Justice is not just a matter of relationships between human beings. There is also the justice of God.

Of course, we know that God is a just judge who allots reward and punishment in accord with our behavior in our earthly life. But that's not all. God doesn't only evaluate us at the end of our lives. He also makes us just here and now. In his generosity, he puts us to rights with himself by giving us his own life to live. He makes us righteous as he is righteous by making us holy as he is holy. God justifies us.

Human justice is different from the justice that God confers on us, yet the two are not totally dissimilar. Our determination to deal appropriately with one another as members of one human family is a reflection of God's desire to deal with us as members of his family. By striving as Christian believers to be just, we try to do for one another what God wants to do for us all.

One of the most eloquent passages in the Bible about justice (in all of its meanings) is in the forty-second chapter of Isaiah (vv. 1–4). God is describing his special servant. Christian tradition has seen these words as speaking of Christ.

> Behold my servant, whom I uphold, my chosen one in whom my soul delights. I have put my Spirit upon him. He will bring forth justice to the nations. He will not cry out or lift up his voice, or make it heard in the street. A bruised reed he will not break, and a dimly burning wick he will not quench. He will faithfully

bring forth justice. He will not fail or be discouraged till he has established justice in the earth....

Christ was sent to bring forth justice, to enable each of us to receive and give everything that God meant us to receive and give, as members of God's family and as members of the human family. Yet the work of Christ was not finished when his earthly life was over. He left behind him a whole community of people who were to continue his mission. They, too, were to be God's beloved servants. They, too, were to be engaged in bringing forth justice.

When Christian believers engage in the pursuit of justice, they are doing more than looking after their own rights, more than seeing that they get what's coming to them. They are doing more than collaborating to bring about a world in which people can live peaceably together. When people of faith strive to deal with rights and responsibilities, many-sided as they are, they are carrying out the mission of the loving and living Christ. That may be the most important reason of all for us to work at bringing forth justice.

What do I think of when I hear the word justice?

What aspects of my life involve being just?

How important is justice in my life?

1

God's Creation:
Who Owns the Garden?

*I*n this and the next four chapters, we will be dealing with basic principles. My purpose is to outline the realities that lie at the foundation of our relationships with one another and with God and to show that justice is not so much a matter of laws, rules, and human customs as of acting in accord with the way things were made to be.

These five basic principles are religious principles, to be sure, but they are also operative in the social and economic philosophy that underlies much of contemporary human society. This is not because contemporary human society is explicitly religious but rather because social and economic thinkers have reflected on what human beings are and have come up with many of the same answers that we find in our Christian faith. The answers are not exactly the same in both contexts, of course, but they both are based on the same realities.

These five principles are interrelated, as we will see in the chapters that follow. Together they form an underpinning of foundational justice on which answers to more specific questions of rights and obligations have to be built.

The most basic of these principles is found at the very beginning of the Bible: "In the beginning God created the heavens and the earth." The earthly reality in which we find ourselves is not of our own making. It came from God, who called it into being very carefully, as the creation account in Genesis makes very clear. God created it to be good—a friendly reality, not a gathering of hostile forces warring against each other. Each component has its part to play in the plan that God had from the beginning for this world that he created.

Humankind has its part to play, too. God tells the man and woman that he has created that they are to have dominion over creation and use the other creatures for their sustenance and development.

But it's still God's creation. God made it for God's purposes. We are merely tenants, called to live as happily and productively as we can while respecting the handiwork of our heavenly landlord. Someone has remarked that, if there were a deed of ownership for the Garden of Eden, there wouldn't be any human name on it, only God's.

Adam and Eve messed things up, as we know, but the basic plan remains the same. The whole of creation is for all of humanity to enjoy in accord with God's love for us human creatures.

This basic insight into the nature of creation is reflected in contemporary concerns for ecology and responsible stewardship. Even nonbelievers acknowledge that the world's resources are not there to do with as we please, to use up or to pollute, to destroy or fritter away through inattention. The world is not ours but is given to us in trust to be used in a way that respects the uniqueness of each creature and the needs of future human generations. It is not right to misuse the world because the world really doesn't belong to any of us individually. This is an important aspect of the theology of creation expressed in nonreligious terms.

All of this raises some fundamental questions about a fundamental element of justice: private property. We know instinctively that there is a distinction between "mine" and "yours." All we have to do to verify that is to listen to children at play or watch two neighbors fighting over who is supposed to cut the grass next to the driveway.

There have been those who thought that private ownership of property is wrong, or at least inappropriate. The Communists, for example, organized a whole social system on the presumption that basic economic resources should be owned not by individuals but by the state. There are dozens of examples of small communities (including the early Christian community in Jerusalem) in which all things were held in common, in which everything belonged to everybody. None of these systems or communities has lasted very long, with the exception of congregations of women and men religious in which each member has voluntarily taken a vow of poverty. For the general run of humankind, private property is a necessity that lies at the very roots of civilized living, and society simply can't exist without it.

There are a number of reasons why human beings have to have some personal ownership of the things they need or use in their day-to-day lives. For one thing, it makes for greater peace and quiet in society. There will not be fights every day on front porches if I know that this is my house and that is your house. Private property offers incentives for work and creativity. Why should I work hard at my business if I am not any better off at the end than the fellow who sits on a park bench all day? Private property also clarifies who is responsible for what and thus guarantees that things get done. People take better care of their own cars than they do of company cars. Basically, private property provides a kind of safe haven in which human beings can live their lives in peace with one another with the realization that their own personhood has space for development, that their own achievements will be respected, and that those they love will benefit from their care.

This is why systems of justice make such elaborate provision for protecting private property. There are laws against theft, robbery, fraud, and trespass, laws about the transfer of real estate, laws about banking. There can be no justice unless what is mine is really mine and what is yours is really yours. Human society cannot survive unless everybody's private property is protected from harm or misappropriation by others.

But there are limits. It would not be just, for example, for one individual to own all the coal or all the water in the world. It would not be just for a few merchants to control a country's food supply. These extremes are unjust because they would violate the rights of others to enjoy the share of the world's goods that they need in order to survive and flourish as human beings.

God gave the whole world for the use and sustenance of all of us. The bishops at the Second Vatican Council spoke of the common purpose of created things ("the universal destination of earthly goods") and taught that the right to have a share of earthly goods sufficient for oneself and one's family applies to everyone (see *Pastoral Constitution on the Church in the Modern World*, no. 69). Pope John Paul II puts the same thing more concretely when he says that private property is under a "social mortgage" (see *Sollicitudo Rei Socialis*, no. 42). If our house is mortgaged, it means that we don't own it purely and simply. The bank owns it, at least in part. Similarly, our private property has a mortgage on it, and that mortgage is constituted by the needs of other human beings.

For that reason, it is not unjust for the government to take away some of our private property in taxes to help provide clean air and water for everybody or to send food to starving people in Somalia. It is not unjust to redistribute wealth through inheritance taxes so that the basic means of maintaining human life don't end up in the hands of a few. In fact, if I am dying of hunger through no fault of my own, it is not unjust for me to break into your house to get something to eat. I have a right to what I need in order to survive.

All that still leaves us with many questions. At what point does government interference with private property become itself unjust? Am I, as an individual, obliged to feed every hungry person that I meet? Is it just for me to buy up all the houses on the street to protect my own property values? If it is unjust for one person to own all the world's coal, would it be just for one nation to control all the world's gold or radium? What about people who are unwilling to contribute to the world through their work? What about people who are unable to contribute? There are multiple aspects to be considered in each of these questions, and there are dozens more questions. But the principles that have to come into play as we face the questions are clear.

Justice is the strong and firm will to give to each what is his or her due. All human beings have the right to what they need in order to live a humane existence. It is their due because God gave us the world for all of us to enjoy. What is mine is indeed mine, but only up to a certain point, and that point is determined by the urgent needs of others.

Just Christians know whose name is on the deed and act accordingly.

What private property do I have? What does it contribute to my life?

Is it possible to have too much?

How do I feel about paying my taxes?

2

Human Dignity:
Who Do You Think You Are?

A second foundational principle of justice is human dignity. In a way, this principle is a specification, a sharper focusing of the principle of creaturehood that we dealt with in the previous chapter. Just as all creation exists for God's purposes and belongs to God and may not simply be used up or thrown away, so also human beings exist because God has called them into being on his terms and for his reasons and must be respected as such.

The word *dignity* means worth or value. When we speak of the principle of human dignity, we mean that every human being has a unique worth or value that nobody can take away and that everybody is called to respect. Each of us has a right to receive respect from others and an obligation to give respect to others simply because we are what God has made us to be.

Scripture expresses this dignity or worth when it tells us that God created us in his own divine image (Gn 1:26f.). We are not like the other creatures of the world. We have a particular value of our own.

The Second Vatican Council says that humankind is the only creature that God willed for itself (see *Pastoral Constitution on the Church in the Modern World*, no. 24). All the other creatures in the world exist for the use of human beings, to feed them or clothe them or give them pleasure because of their beauty and variety. Human beings exist for themselves, simply because God wanted them to be. One might say that, while other creatures exist to gladden human hearts, human beings exist to gladden the heart of God. Our worth consists in this special value that God has conferred on us and that no one can take away.

This religious truth is reflected in social and political terms in the basic insight that gave rise to our American Revolution. In the Declaration of Independence the founding fathers said that it is self-evident that "all men are created equal" and "that they are endowed by their Creator with certain unalienable rights." That is to say, every human being has a dignity that exists prior to any conferral of rights by government, and that dignity can never be obliterated by any human power.

This human worth, whether viewed from a theological or from a sociopolitical perspective, does not depend on achievement. It is not the case that we must each prove our worth and then we have a right to be respected by other people. Human worth does not depend on usefulness; society does not have the right to do away with those who seem to contribute nothing to the common good. It does not depend on wealth or the social standing of our family or even on our appropriate behavior in society. The dignity of our being human is a given that precedes any worthy action of our own, a given that cannot be forfeited by any evil that we may do.

Christian social thinkers are fond of saying that human life is always an end in itself, never a means to something else. This is another way of saying that the value of human beings depends not on what they can do but on what they are. Every human being is important just for being a human being. No human being is expendable, an object to be thrown away if it doesn't work right.

This inborn human dignity is easy to see sometimes. We

look at the good and productive people around us and can appreciate their worth. Our family and friends are important to us, and we know that they are also important to the Lord. We admire great political leaders and scientists and artists. Their worth and value is obvious. It's often otherwise with less attractive people. What about the crack dealer and the professional welfare cheat and the child abuser? What about the swindler who steals the resources of widows and orphans? What about Hitler and Stalin? All these people have an unalienable human worth that precedes the good or the evil they may have done. There is a basic commonality of human worth that the best of us cannot earn for ourselves and the worst of us cannot destroy in ourselves. That fundamental human dignity calls for the respect of the rest of us.

Where does justice come into all this? If justice is the strong and firm will to give to each what is his or her due, and if every human being is gifted with a worth that can never be lost, then it is clear that a certain level of respect and reverence is due to every human being. We have a claim on one another to be treated with care not just for what we have or have not done but for what we are. Given the fundamental nature of human dignity, given the importance of that human dignity in every sort of interpersonal relationship, given the claim that the dignity of others has on us and that our dignity has on others, one might well say that one of the most basic purposes of justice is to protect and foster human dignity. To put this in another way, the fundamental question of justice is the question of what we owe to the humanity of others and they to ours.

First and foremost is personal inviolability. Given our human value, our fundamental right is the right to life. It is unjust for me to take the life of another human being simply because his or her life is not mine to take. "Thou shalt not kill" is not only the fifth commandment of God but also the basic requirement for human life together in society. Once human life becomes expendable or vulnerable, the value of everyone's life has been put in jeopardy.

There are questions in our society about this most basic principle of justice. The questions deal with both ends of the spectrum of human life. Is it appropriate to kill an unborn child? Not if that child is a human being. Is it appropriate to kill a dying person, to put him or her out of misery by providing a speedy death? Not if that sick person is a human being. Our worth does not depend on individual viability at the beginning of life or on productivity and freedom from suffering at it end. There is also the question of capital punishment. The Church teaches that society may, indeed, execute someone guilty of criminal behavior, but only if that is the only way for society to defend the lives of others. Popular sentiment says that the criminal deserves to die for what he or she has done because there is no longer any human worth there. That sort of thinking is not in accord with what we believe about human dignity.

Personal inviolability is not merely a matter of respecting the life of the other, however. It also involves respecting his or her bodily integrity, privacy, self-respect, and good name. It is not merely uncharitable to humiliate or demean another human being. It is also unjust because we are not respecting the rights of that person. We are not giving what is his or her due.

This may be the appropriate place to say something about that subdivision of justice that we call criminal justice. It is right to call people to account for the injury they have inflicted on the human dignity of others. But that call to account must also respect the dignity of the accused person. It must provide means for the accused to defend him- or herself, it must presume the innocence of the accused until guilt is proven, and, if punishment is to be inflicted, the punishment must not violate the inherent human worth of the criminal. It is unjust to treat even criminals like animals.

When we say that justice calls for universal respect for the dignity of every human person, we are also saying that every human person has a right to those things that are necessary to maintain a decent human existence. According to the United Nations' "Universal Declaration of Human Rights," this includes the right to appropriate housing, medical care, and education. How such things are to be provided and by whom are complex questions that we will have more to say about later. But they are to be provided as a right, not because those who need them are contributors to the common well-being in some way or other, but because they are human beings.

Human life cannot flourish without justice. Unless we give and get what is due, we live in a state of disruption and deprivation. The most basic thing that is due to us, the most basic thing that is due to others is respect for the worth of our common humanity.

Sometimes when two people are having a hot argument, one will say, "Just who do you think you are?" It's a question that we all have to address, even apart from arguments. Just Christians know who and what they are, and they know who and what their brothers and sisters are, too.

Who and what do I think that I am?

Why do I respect the people I respect?

Whom do I respect the least? Why?

3

Human Responsibility:
Who's in Charge Here?

We have seen that we all have a right to that share of the world's goods that we need in order to live a truly human life. We have also seen that every human being has the right to be respected simply for being human and that there is no earthly power that can abrogate that right to human dignity. But how is all that to happen? How are these basic rights of ours to be put into operation and protected? Who is responsible for all this? The answer is simple: we are.

When God settled Adam in the garden, God gave Adam the responsibility to cultivate it and care for it (see Gn 2:15). After Adam and Eve sinned, God told them that the task of cultivating the world would now be a toilsome one (see Gn 3:17), but the task was still theirs. Human beings are responsible for what goes on in the world. While God is still very much an interested party and intends the world to operate according to the principles on which it was created, the responsibility for the day-to-day running of it is ours.

This concept of human responsibility is reflected in civil society as well. In the Declaration of Independence, one of the unalienable rights that the founders said was self-evident was the right to the pursuit of happiness. Human beings have the right to work for their own well-being, and if they have the right, they also have the responsibility.

In times past this right and responsibility to work for human happiness was seen in a narrower way than it is today. Certain things were simply taken as givens that were not subject to change: social standing, the distribution of wealth, the structures of authority—that which we today would call "the system." The king and his agents saw to it that people had what was coming to them and looked after the development of the land's resources. The king's will was looked upon as expressing the will of God. Ordinary people were not thought to be equipped to deal with these matters.

It was only a few hundred years ago that people began to realize that the system could be changed, that it wasn't all that it should be, that the rights and responsibilities of kings to govern, to defend rights, and to promote prosperity could and should be shared by others, that God didn't have to work through royalty. We now realize that, if things can be improved, if the goods of the world can be better used and more fairly distributed, if human dignity can be more effectively fostered, it is up to ordinary human beings, because of their inborn human capabilities, to see that the improvements take place. If there is injustice, if the rights of human beings are being violated, it is up to other human beings, because of their inborn responsibilities, to do something about it. Ordinary human beings can change things—for themselves and for others. Ordinary human beings can and must be the agents of God in bringing forth justice.

If my neighbor trespasses on my property, I can pray for help from the Lord, but I also can demand the intervention of the police. If I have been defrauded of my wages, I can call to heaven for vengeance, but I also can bring suit against my employer. If whole categories of persons are suffering discrimination, they can call to the God of the oppressed to look out for them, but they also can work to see to it that laws are passed to protect them. The Lord is not absent from the world. God's will for creation and humankind is the same as it has always been. He works in ways that we neither see nor understand. But the Lord also works through the agency of human beings.

But having established the principle of human responsibility, we still have lots of questions to answer. Is everybody in charge of everything? How do we determine who is responsible for what? Is government supposed to do it all? Who decides who is to govern and how?

Most modern countries are governed democratically. That is to say, the persons who are in charge of bringing forth justice for the nation at large are chosen by the nation's people. The particulars vary from place to place, but we seem to have learned that government is most effective when the governed have something to say about who governs them and about how government should work. This implies that the people themselves have some idea about justice, rights, and responsibility and are willing to take the trouble to think about what is needed in their society to promote justice most effectively. Having everybody vote is not particularly meaningful if nobody knows what he or she is voting about.

It would seem, then, that for the individual a basic responsibility in society is to take an interest in what is going on and, if nothing else, to vote in a conscientious and thoughtful fashion. We cannot say that we are doing our part for justice if we refuse to become involved in the process that provides the means for justice to be done for ourselves and for others.

Obviously, there will be differences of opinion. Justice is not a simple thing, and the questions that government has to deal with often admit of more than one answer. All just Christians will not have the same ideas about all the specifics, but they may not say that the pursuit of justice in the land is not their concern.

All this is not to say, however, that the whole project of justice and human well-being should be carried out by government. Some parts of it, like the nurture and education of children, must be taken care of in the family. Some of it can be carried out through voluntary groupings like labor unions, private schools, and social agencies sponsored by churches. Some of it is indeed the task of government, but there are different levels of government, and not everything can be or should be taken care of by government at the highest level.

In this context, there is a wonderfully wise principle that occurs frequently in the Church's social teaching: the principle of subsidiarity. This principle teaches that justice and human well-being are best looked after at the most immediate level. People should be allowed to provide for themselves as much as possible, given the needs that they are dealing with. They must have the opportunity to exercise their human responsibility for themselves to the greatest possible degree. It is wrong for government to take over things that people can do for themselves in the family or in voluntary associations. Yet, at the same time, government must be prepared to deal with issues that smaller groupings cannot handle. Government should not tell a father what kind of job he must work at to support his family, how his children are to be dressed, or whether he can belong to a union or not. Federal government should not decide whether there is to be a traffic light at a country crossroads. On the other hand, federal government should not expect county commissioners to put together an interstate highway system. What kind of government is a just government? The kind that allows the fullest exercise of individual human responsibility, a government that is as small as possible but big enough to look after the demands of the common good. Obviously, not everyone will agree about what this means in practice, but the principle is an important one because it teaches that justice is the responsibility of us all.

Justice doesn't just happen. Providing a fair share of the earth's goods to everybody, protecting the human dignity of each person, making it possible for individuals and families to grow toward the fulfillment of what God has made possible for them in the world is a many-sided project. How is it all going to happen? It's going to happen through individuals who are just, who have the strong and firm will to see that each person has what is his or her due. We are not all statesmen. We don't all hold political office. Most of us are not rich or influential. But all of us have the opportunity to practice justice and to seek for justice in greater or lesser degrees. And if we have the opportunity to practice and seek for justice, we also have the responsibility to do so.

Who's in charge of justice around here? Just Christians know that they are.

For whom and for what do I consider myself responsible?

Whom do I consider responsible for me, and for what?

To what extent is government involved in my life? Is this degree of involvement appropriate?

4

Human Solidarity: Who Is My Neighbor?

We have seen that everybody has a claim on enough of the world's goods to enable each to live a decent human life and that this claim is based on our inherent worth as human beings. We have also seen that the task of protecting this claim and of seeing that it is fulfilled belongs to us all. We all share responsibility for bringing forth justice.

In this chapter we will discuss the *extent* of that responsibility. For whom and for what am I responsible?

The basics are obvious. We have responsibility for those who constitute the immediate circle of our lives. God's word tells us that we must honor our father and our mother and that we must love our neighbor as ourselves (see Ex 20:12; Lv 19:18; Lk 10:27). Justice, giving to each what is his or her due, is meaningless unless we respect first of all the rights and the dignity of those who are closest to us and unless they respect ours.

But none of us lives in a hermetically sealed circle. It is true that our family and friends play a major part in our lives, but we also depend on human beings who are more remote from our personal circle, and if we depend on them, they depend on us. The circle of our lives includes our neighborhood and our workplace. It includes our town and our country. As human knowledge and ingenuity have developed, we have also become involved with people all over the world. The clothes we wear may have been made in Korea, and the cars we drive, in Japan. If there is a war in the Middle East, it affects the price of gas at our local filling station. Working conditions in Mexico have their effect on the job market in the Midwest. The circle of our lives ultimately includes the whole circle of human reality.

This universal inclusiveness is reflected in the world's political realm. Just as no human individual can live in a closed circle of family and friends, no country can be concerned with itself alone, uninvolved with what is going on in the rest of the world. That awareness has given rise to the twentieth century's efforts at bringing countries together for the sake of worldwide justice. The United Nations organization, limited and ineffective as it may sometimes seem, is not a debating society but an eloquent testimony that the context of justice is no longer merely the family or the village or the national state but the world at large.

The mind-set that recognizes this interdependence of all human beings is called "solidarity." Solidarity recognizes a community of values, interests, objectives, and standards. Solidarity can be founded on the awareness that we are all children of God and share God's love as the basis of our human dignity. But an awareness of human solidarity can also be founded on the realization that, from a purely pragmatic perspective, we all need each other and that, therefore, we all have claims on each other. In *Sollicitudo Rei Socialis* (no. 38), Pope John Paul II says that solidarity is a moral category that involves "a firm and persevering determination to commit oneself to the common good; ... to the good of all and of each individual, because we are all really responsible for all." Solidarity is justice writ large.

What does it mean in practice to say that we are all really responsible for all? For one thing, it means that we may not look on our lives only as our personal, individual concern.

Looking out for number one and for number one only is simply wrong because it involves walking away from our responsibilities toward everybody else and denying their responsibilities toward us. We Americans have idealized the rugged individual, the person who goes it alone, who makes his or her way with the least possible help from others and who, at the end, takes satisfaction in the fact that he or she owes nothing to anybody. This ideal is not only unrealistic but also unjust because it disregards what we necessarily receive from others and, therefore, what we owe to them, whether we like it or not. Nobody can live a completely solitary life, and the measure of our humanity is not how little we rely on others but how widely we are willing to extend the circle of our embrace to those around us.

Does this mean that I am personally responsible for the improvement of working conditions in Bangkok or for sorting out the ethnic conflicts in the Balkans? Yes and no.

Justice is the strong and firm will to give to each what is his or her due. My obligations in justice depend on what I am able to give toward what is due to others. These "others" stand around us in a series of concentric circles.

First of all, I am responsible for myself. It is not just for me to expect others to provide what I can provide for myself. If I am able to work and if there are jobs available, it is wrong for me to sit back and wait for the unemployment check to come in the mail. That's little better than theft.

Then I am responsible for my family: for parents if they are in need, for spouse and children to the extent that they depend on me. Responsibility is determined in large part by our degree of connectedness with these "others." For the same reason, I owe help and consideration to my friends. These are the closest to me and the ones for whom I can do the most, so they are the ones to whom I owe the most.

This much is obvious. But as the circles widen, the temptation to back off increases. Do I owe something to those who are "different": persons of other races, immigrants, those who are poorer (or richer) than I am? Indeed I do, to the extent that I am able to see that their rights and their human dignity are respected. At very least, I owe my dues as a fellow member of society: dues of money in taxes, dues of concern for their human worth, dues of participation in determining how justice is to be brought forth in the political units we share. My obligations toward myself and my family and friends may make it difficult for me to get involved much beyond these minimums with the needs of those who are "different," but I may not say that I have no responsibility for them.

It is the same with the widest circle of all, the worldwide circle of our common humanity. Obviously, one individual cannot unravel the problems of inequity in the global economy. One individual cannot bring reconciliation to conflicts that have been going on for hundreds of years. But one individual can encourage others who have greater influence and expertise to keep looking for solutions. One individual can raise his or her voice to keep saying that he or she, together with others, will not be content with a general political or social posture that refuses to deal with the needs of the rest of the world. What we have to offer in this widest circle may be little, but that little is what we owe.

One of the reasons that concern for social problems is so frustrating, whether they be the problems of our local community or of our country or of the world at large, is that they are so complex. We want quick and clear solutions that put things to rights in short order. In these contexts, such solutions are simply not available. Sometimes literally nobody knows what can be done. But that doesn't justify giving up the search. Justice is difficult, and part of the pursuit of justice is keeping at it, even when we don't know what the answer is. One thing that is always clear, however, is that justice will never be brought forth if nobody cares.

Exclusion and divisiveness are the grounds on which the abuse of human dignity grows, the grounds on which injustice thrives. To the extent that I exclude human beings from my concern, however distant those human beings may seem, however ineffective my concern may appear in the general picture, I have undermined the solidarity that is a basic principle of justice.

When the legal expert (see Lk 10:25 ff.) asked Jesus, "Who is my neighbor?" it was taken for granted that we have obligations toward the neighbor. The issue was to identify the neighbor. Who is included in the definition? How wide is the circle? Just Christians know that the circle includes everybody who is in need, and that every human being has need of all the rest.

How much do I care about what goes on in the world around me?

What specific things can I do to influence national policy?

Whom do I look on as my neighbor? What difference does that make to the neighbor and to me?

5

Care for the Poor:
Stand Over There?

We have been dealing with the foundational principles of justice. We have considered God's ownership of creation, our human dignity, human responsibility, and human solidarity. Each principle has its own force, yet all are interconnected. Our fifth principle also involves the other four and is, in a way, a particular application of them to a special group of people, the poor.

The New Testament has a lot to say about the poor. Jesus invited people to sell what they had and give to the poor (Mt 19:21). He spoke with approval of the poor widow who gave to God the little that she had (Mk 12:42f.). He called the poor happy and said that the kingdom of God belongs to them (Lk 6:20). One of the signs of his messianic mission was that the good news was being proclaimed to the poor (Lk 7:22). Part of the mission of St. Paul was to remind the new churches of their responsibility for the poor in Jerusalem (see Rom 15:26; 2 Cor 8:2; Gal 2:10).

Throughout the centuries that followed New Testament times, the Church was always involved in various kind of assistance to the poor: material assistance, education, health care. In our own time, Pope Paul VI spoke of the gospel's instruction about "a preferential respect due to the poor and the special situation they have in society" (*Octogesima Adveniens*, no. 23).

Care for the poor is not just a religious activity. Civil

society looks after the poor, or the potentially poor, through all kinds of social welfare programs: Social Security, Aid to Dependent Children, Section Eight Housing, minimum wage laws, and the like. This suggests that looking out for the poor is not just a matter of religious conviction but of fundamental justice as well.

Before we can examine the reason why care for the poor is a fundamental principle of justice, we have to be clear about who the poor are. The poor are not just those who have less money than other people. If that were the sole criterion, we could all be called poor because practically all of us have less money than somebody else, perhaps even less than we think we need. In the context with which we are dealing here, the poor are those who lack the basic necessities of human life and who are unable to do anything about their lack. They are those who are somehow left out of the system. They are the marginalized, the powerless. These are the women and men who have a claim for preferential respect and special attention.

Why? Because, for one thing, they do not have their rightful share of the blessings of creation that God meant us all to share. Consequently, their fundamental human dignity is threatened. Moreover, because of the situation in which they find themselves, they are not able to exercise a rightful degree of responsibility for themselves and for others and often find themselves outside the embrace of human solidarity, whether as doers of justice or as its recipients. They live in a situation that is fundamentally unjust.

The poor also have a right to preferential respect and special attention because they can so easily be written off. If we are not particularly and carefully attentive to the rights of the poor, we may ourselves become perpetrators of or collaborators in basic injustice.

The poor in society are like disabled members of a family. They require more attention from the other members because of what they are unable to do for themselves. Their claim on this special attention is not what they have contributed in the past or might still contribute in the future, but merely that they are members of the family who can't make it on their own.

People are often tempted to disdain the poor. "I made it on my own. Why can't they? They could work if they really wanted to." It's not unheard of for people to equate poor people with bad people. Comments and thoughts like these are wrong because most of the time they are simply not true. It may be the case that some people, through their own fault, are unwilling to contribute what they can to society. But for the vast majority of the poor, the question is not being unwilling but being unable, unable for physical or psychological reasons, unable because they have not had opportunities for education, unable because economic or technological developments have passed them by, unable because our society simply doesn't have a place for them. This doesn't make them bad people, it simply makes them poor people. As for any of us having "made it on our own," it might be interesting to know what our lives would have been with different parents, if we had been born somewhere else or at a different time, if we had not gotten the right breaks when we needed them. Most of us owe much more than we have earned, and we repay that debt, in part, by helping others get what we already have.

One of the reasons that we are tempted to write off the poor is that the solutions to their problems are so complicated. We have learned that government programs sometimes seem to cause more difficulties than they solve, that the economic and social cost of dealing with poverty is extremely high, that good people often differ about what can and should be done. The easiest thing is to say that it's somebody else's fault or that there are no solutions and then walk away to continue to enjoy what is ours.

But we are not allowed to walk away, because we are in solidarity with the poor. Their basic human rights and human dignity are the same as ours. We are responsible for the well-being of others even as we are responsible for the well-being of ourselves and of those who are closest to us.

Basically, we are called to give particular attention to the poor precisely because the poor lack power of their own. They are unable to exercise their rights and their responsibilities because of the system in which they find themselves. Consequently, it is up to those who enjoy a measure of power to modify the system so that those who are now outsiders are able to participate in it. We will be saying more about this later when we deal with social justice. At this point it may be enough to recall that the measure of a society's health is how it treats its poor.

When we say that we owe preferential respect and special attention to the poor, we are not saying that the poor should not be held accountable for their participation in society according to the same standards as everybody else. Rather, we are saying that they require respect and attention so as to be able to take their appropriate part in the social system and thus not only benefit from it but contribute to it.

When we think of our obligations to the poor, we must not allow ourselves to think in terms of "them" and "us." To one extent or another, we are all dependent, all disabled, all without power, all underproductive. Ultimately, we all stand poor before the Lord. Unless we are able to acknowledge that poverty, we will be unable to understand and accept the generosity and love that the Lord offers us. This is why Jesus says that the kingdom of God belongs to the poor. Likewise, unless we extend ourselves to do what we can to deal with the needs of our economically and socially poor sisters and brothers, we have no right to expect that the Lord will extend himself to deal with our poverty. Concern for the poor keeps all of us aware of who and what we ourselves are. It may well be that those who are comparatively well-off in the world need the poor as much as the poor need them. It is certainly the case that those who commit themselves to working for the poor generally find that they receive much more than they give.

Concern for the poor has always been a challenge for the followers of Christ. There seem to have been problems even in the early Church. In the Letter of James (2:1 ff.), the author takes his listeners to task for making distinctions between rich and poor in the community assembly. It's wrong, he says, to invite the well-dressed and bejewelled members to come up front and take the best seats and to tell the poor member, "Stand over there." The just Christian knows that the only appropriate arrangement is for all of us to stand together.

Do I consider myself poor or rich? Why?

Whom do I consider poor? Why?

What do I have to offer to the poor? What do those whom I consider poor have to offer to me?

6

Rights: What's Coming to Me

We have seen that justice is the determination to give to each what is his or her due. We have also seen that what is due to each is fundamentally determined by our status as sharers in God's creation, gifted with human dignity, each of us bearing a share of responsibility for ourselves and for our brothers and sisters everywhere, especially for those less able to look out for themselves. Now it is time to look at justice in greater detail.

Justice has to do with rights and obligations. Generally speaking, rights involve what is owing to me and obligations involve what I owe to others. In this chapter we will deal with rights, and in the next with obligations. Of course, the two can't really be separated because rights and obligations are relative to each other; every right of mine involves some level of duty or obligation on the part of someone else, and vice versa.

A right is a claim to something, something about me that others must respect. It is what is owed to me, my due. For example, if I work for a certain number of hours, my employer owes me a certain sum of money in wages. I have a claim on the employer. I have a right to be paid.

We each have all kinds of rights, and they arise from several different sources. Some rights arise from the simple fact that we are human beings. These are what we call basic human rights. The United Nations in 1948 issued a "Universal Declaration of Human Rights" based on "the

inherent dignity... of all members of the human family."
Pope John XXIII in 1963 offered a similar list in *Pacem in Terris* (nos. 11-26), as did Pope John Paul II in his address to the United Nations in 1979 (no. 13). The human rights listed in these various sources include the right to life and bodily integrity; to food, clothing, shelter, rest, and medical care; to freedom in the worship of God and in the pursuit of truth; to private property, work, free assembly, and participation in public affairs; to the resources needed to establish a family; and to education and participation in the benefits of culture. All of these, and others besides, constitute a true claim in justice that each human being has on humanity at large, not because of any achievement on the part of the individual or any specific action on the part of government, but simply by reason of being human. They are our natural human rights.

Other rights arise from our belonging to a certain society or nation that grants the rights. In our country, for example, all citizens not otherwise excepted have the right to vote once they are eighteen years old. This right is granted by the Constitution and its various amendments. The right could be further expanded or limited, but once the appropriate government body has determined what the right is, each qualified citizen has a claim to exercise it that no one may inhibit.

Still other rights come through agreement between individuals. When I go to the drug store, I enter an implicit contract with the owner to pay the price for the articles I wish to buy. Once I have paid, those articles are mine and nobody can take them away from me. I have established a claim that others must respect. I have a right to them.

Rights are basic to human existence because they identify and protect that which is necessary for my life as a human participant in creation. If there is no such thing as a right, then each of us is at the mercy of those who are stronger or smarter or more aggressive than we are. Rights provide a kind of personal inviolability for each of us, the fundamental grounds of respect that we each and all need if we are to live together in human society.

But all this is only the beginning. Once we have passed beyond these basic concepts of rights, their sources, and their significance, the project of bringing forth justice has only begun.

Perhaps the most fundamental challenge of justice is the task of identifying rights in practice. Sometimes it's easy, as when we leave the drug store with the articles we have paid for. I have a right to those articles, to all of them and to no other ones. If somebody challenges me as I leave the store, I can show them the sales slip and prove that these things are now mine. Similarly, I have the right to bodily integrity, so it is obviously a violation of my rights for somebody to hit me over the head as I walk down the street. If somebody does that, I can go to the police and the person who injured me will be punished. My rights can be protected because they are clear.

Sometimes things are not so clear. What are my rights when a neighbor's tree branch falls on my roof during a storm? Are my rights being violated when the air hammers being used to fix the street outside make it impossible for me to do my work? We have attorneys and courts and whole bodies of law to help clarify issues like these where there seems to be a conflict of rights.

Then there are our basic human rights. The general conviction of humankind as well as the direct and clear teaching of several popes tells me that every human being has a right to food, clothing, and shelter. What does that mean in practice? Do I have the right to take what I want from a shopping mall on the basis of these human rights? Obviously not. But if these rights have any practical meaning, there must be some way to exercise and protect them. This is where government has a responsibility to exercise. Government has to determine how each citizen is to attain an appropriate share of what he or she needs for a human life. The degree of government involvement and the specifics of various human rights programs are matters that form a large part of the political and social discussion that takes place in the life of each nation.

There is also the question of rights between nations. When there is a dispute about what is owed to whom on an international scale, the question of justice becomes even more complex. Generally, there is some right on both sides. But who is to determine what the right is? Who is to enforce the right once it has been identified? Historically, the ordinary means of enforcing national rights has been war, the basic presumption of which is that the group that is able to enforce its will on the others must have had more right on its side. This approach is proving ever more unsatisfactory as wars become more and more destructive. In addition to that, however, the presumption that might makes right in the long run is one that has frightening implications for the pursuit of any authentic justice.

A large part of the project of bringing forth justice, therefore, is the task of clarifying what the rights are, how they are to be exercised, and how they are to be defended. Rights seem to be clearest at the most particular level, that of interaction between individuals. As the context becomes larger and the rights more general, the questions of identification and implementation become more difficult. It's easier to determine my right to my wages than it is to determine how the poor are to be enabled to exercise their right to decent housing. In some of our later chapters we will look at the various contexts in which justice is practiced. At this point we can only observe that the difficulty of bringing about justice does not absolve us from the effort.

One last observation is important. Rights exist not just to protect my own individual humanity but the common good of us all. Consequently, as I defend and exercise my personal rights, I have to be aware that there is a larger dimension. I have a right to private property, for example, but that right is limited by the needs of others. I have a right to do what I want in my house, but that right is limited by the neighbors' right to peace and quiet. If I begin to look on my rights as affecting only me, I have turned rights into an instrument of selfishness rather than a means of assuring access to that which belongs to all of us together. Rights are part of God's providence for me, but they are also part of God's providence for everyone.

There is an old Latin proverb that is relevant here: *summum ius, summa iniuria,* extreme claims of right constitute extreme injustice. Just Christians know that individual rights always involve community rights. The issue is not merely what I have coming to me but also what we have coming to us.

What rights are most precious to me?

Have my rights ever been violated? What was my reaction?

How am I involved in protecting the human rights of others?

7

Obligations: What I Owe

We have seen that justice is a matter of rights and obligations and that the two are in relationship with one another. The practice of justice consists in clarifying and exercising the implications of this relationship. In the last chapter we spoke of rights. Now we will deal with obligations.

If rights only exist in the abstract, they don't mean very much. For example, if I have a right to my wages, somebody has to have the obligation to pay me. If I have the right to vote, there has to be some means for enforcing that right. Somebody, either an individual or some agency of government, must have the obligation of seeing that I can exercise that right. If, as a human being, I have the right to basic food and shelter, there must be a corresponding obligation somewhere to ensure that I get what's owing to me. Otherwise, justice becomes a matter of pious desire, something that everybody is in favor of but nobody has to do anything about.

When we speak of obligations in the context of justice, we are speaking of responsibilities for rights. Who bears such responsibilities? We all do. We all owe. In the various contexts of justice, we are all, in varying degrees responsible for the rights of one another because justice is essentially communal. It takes at least two to have justice. But even as one of the basic challenges of justice is to determine in detail what our rights are, so also we must deal with the challenge of clarifying our obligations. For whom and for what are we specifically responsible? Who owes what to whom?

Just as rights are clearest at the most particular level, so are obligations. If you are my employer, it is you who owe me my wages. If you are in charge of the local civil rights commission, it is you (and your colleagues) who have the obligation to see that I can exercise my right to vote. But as rights become more general, so do the obligations to defend them. Who is responsible for seeing that every human being has his or her basic needs for food and shelter taken care of? The principles we dealt with earlier make it clear that all of us share that obligation. But when an obligation is shared by everybody, there is a danger that it will not be carried out by anybody. At the very least, the individual's pursuit of justice must include some degree of practical concern for these more general rights that cannot be defended exclusively on a person-to-person basis. The temptation is to say, "Let George do it." But the principles of human dignity, human responsibility, and human solidarity, not to mention our obligation of care for the poor, keep reminding us that George is not somebody else. George is me.

As we reflect on our obligations in bringing forth justice, on what we owe, there are three important cautions that we need to keep ourselves aware of.

The first is that our obligations in justice are not exclusively matters of legality. Of course I owe this much on my income tax because the legislators have determined by law what my share is in the expenses of running the country. I have an obligation to obey the law, but I am free to take advantage of every possible exemption because they are part of the law, too. But justice has a deeper foundation than law. It is founded on the way God made the world to be, and as I view my obligations in justice, I have to keep in mind not only the detailed requirements of law but also what God intended in creating this world of ours populated by human beings.

Thus, for example, our common humanity obliges us to give something in exchange for what we get from other people by way of goods and services. Reciprocity is part of living together for human beings. It makes possible the sharing of products and talents. It encourages each of us to reach out beyond ourselves and our families and thus extends and tightens the bonds of the human family. The law may determine what we can be charged and in what medium the exchange must take place, but the fundamental obligation to give for what we have received is part of being human and binds us more deeply than the details of specific laws.

Likewise, we owe something to our civic community simply because we are its members. The law may specify certain modes of behavior that are required of all citizens, but the obligation to strive to live together in peace is deeper than the requirements of the law.

If the only obligations we acknowledge are the strict obligations of law, we run the risk of overlooking the basic principles on which both law and human togetherness are founded. We end up doing only the legal minimum, that which the laws can enforce. If that becomes the sole norm of justice, then the soundness and depth of our relationships with one another will be determined by the size of the police force.

The second caution is similar to the first but somewhat broader. Bringing forth justice does not consist in attempting to broaden my rights and narrow my obligations. Justice is more than a commercial transaction in which we buy for as little as possible and sell for as much as we can get. In the last chapter I quoted the Latin proverb *summum ius, summa iniuria*, extreme claims of right constitute extreme injustice. The flip side is true also: minimum willingness to assume obligations makes for minimum justice. The reason is the same: justice is concerned not only with my getting what's coming to me but also with our life together as a human community.

The issue here is maturity. People who are only interested in getting what's coming to them, who see their obligations in the narrowest possible way, are being childish. They see everything in terms of themselves and their desires. Maturity consists in understanding why things are the way they are and how things are meant to be, and acting accordingly. Mature people are those who want what is right not because it is advantageous to them but simply because it is right and because what is right will ultimately be the best for us all. Mature people are those who carry out their obligations not because they must but because they want to.

The third caution is basic to the other two. Obligation is not burden but gift. Justice involves my responsibility for the rights of others. This responsibility implies that I have the capacity and the power to promote the well-being of other human beings. It is my opportunity to share in God's providence in the context of human dignity and human community. God says to us, "I expect you to have an ongoing determination to give to each what is his or her due." To look on this responsibility merely as a matter of observing laws or of giving what we must in order to get what we want is to trivialize God's love for other human beings and to turn our capacity to act as God's agents into self-serving.

If you want to test the validity of this principle, consider parenthood. Parents have heavy obligations in justice to their children. They must feed and clothe them. They must provide housing and education. They must control their behavior. If parents don't do these things, the law will step in to force the parents to live up to their obligations. In return for what parents do, children are expected to show obedience to and reverence for their parents and to take care of them if they are in need. Parents have a right to expect that. The obligations and the rights are very clear. But is that all there is to parenthood? One certainly hopes not. Parenthood also involves a sharing of love and concern, an opportunity to participate in God's loving providence immediately and clearly. Of course it involves responsibility and obligation and law, but before any of that it is gift, gift to the children and gift to the parents themselves.

Justice is always a two-way street. It involves rights: guarantees of personal inviolability that I need in order to live as a human being. It involves obligations: my responsibilities to contribute to the humanity of those around me. I cannot be a fully human being unless I am serious about both my rights and my obligations. Just Christians are those who travel the street confidently, gladly, and gratefully in both directions.

What obligations of justice do I find in my life?

Which obligations do I find most burdensome? Most rewarding?

How would my behavior change if there were no laws?

8

Commutative Justice: A Fair Exchange

We have dealt with the principles that underlie and constitute justice. We have described the basic components of all justice in speaking about rights and obligations. Now it is time to say something about the various kinds of justice, that is, about the various contexts in which we are called to exercise our "strong and firm will to give to each what is his or her due."

The most ordinary and clear kind of justice is commutative justice, the justice of exchange. It is concerned with the rights and obligations of individuals and private social groups in matters of freely formed relationships. Commutative justice comes into play in such relationships as purchase and contract. It involves the right to get what you pay for and the obligation of paying for what you get.

For example, when I fill up the tank of my car at the service station, I may put in twelve gallons of eighty-seven octane gas. The pump shows that I owe $13.68. There is no question about what I owe or to whom I owe it or how I am supposed to pay. Likewise, there is no question about what I have gotten for my money: twelve gallons of eighty-seven octane gas. I pay my bill and go on my way. There has been a complete and fair exchange. The demands of commutative justice are clear and they have been observed.

Similarly, if I enter a contract with the young man down the street to cut my grass, we agree on what I am to pay and what he is to do. Once he has done what he agreed to do, I give him the payment we have agreed on. The contract is concluded, and we are both satisfied because he has gotten my money in exchange for his work and I have gotten his work in exchange for my money. It was a just transaction.

The norm by which commutative justice is measured is strict numerical equality. A just transaction always concludes with equalness, an equality between what was given and what was gotten.

Commutative justice is based on two of our basic principles: the principle of human responsibility and the principle of human dignity. Because we all bear joint responsibility for the development of the creation that God has given us, we must work with each other. No one can live, grow, and develop exclusively on personal resources. There has to be some exchange of what I have for what I need, an exchange that involves what you have for what you need. If that exchange is going to result in benefit to both of us, it has to be a fair exchange. There has to be justice. Otherwise, our attempt to work together will degenerate into a contest in which only the stronger or the smarter or the shrewder can win. Commutative justice is the practice of our common responsibility for creation.

The principle of basic human dignity comes into play also. When I fill up my gas tank, it doesn't matter whether the station manager is somebody I like or not, whether he takes care of his family or not, whether he goes to church on Sunday or not. What matters is whether I get what I paid for. The basic context in the exchange is our common humanity. The manager is a human being who is engaged in the enterprise of human life just as I am, and on that grounds we are equal and must treat each other with the respect that is due between equals.

Given all this, it's easy to see how commutative justice

can be violated. It is violated whenever there is a lack of equality in a transaction. The basic kinds of commutative injustice are fraud, theft, and damage. If I discover that the gas I bought at the filling station was only seventy-five octane, I have suffered an injustice because I did not get what I paid for. I have been defrauded. If I try to weasel out of paying the young man who took care of my lawn by not answering the door when he comes to collect, I am unjust because I did not pay for what I got in accord with what had been agreed. I have stolen from him. If somebody spray paints my housefront on Halloween, that person is unjust to me because he or she has damaged my property and thus diminished its value without giving me anything in return.

Not all kinds of injustice are as clear and plain as the three examples I have just given. Some forms of advertising constitute fraud because they extol the future value of worthless products. The padded expense account is a kind of theft. And when the doctor doesn't tell his patient about the side effects of the medication he prescribes, the patient suffers involuntary and therefore unjust damage.

In instances of injustice, whether they are clear and obvious or the result of deviousness or culpable neglect on the part of someone else, I can have recourse to the processes of law to have the balance restored. I make my complaint in the appropriate forum and the court determines how much I have coming to me to recompense me for my loss. Civil law has an interest in promoting commutative justice between individuals because commutative justice is so fundamentally important for the smooth operation of human society. Our life together would become impossible if we could not be sure that our exchanges with one another were going to be fair. This is why civil law provides not only for the restoration of equality in the exchange but also for punishments for those who have been found guilty of unjust behavior.

These legal processes are not always simple, of course. Those in charge of seeing that justice is done have to verify the facts. They have to determine what was understood, or should have been understood, in the agreement. They have to find out whether what happened was the result of ill will or of ignorance on the part of one or both of the parties. They have to assess damages. These processes may be brief hearings in small claims court to get a seller to provide to the buyer what was promised. They can also be formal court cases that take years and result in multimillion dollar settlements to people who have been injured by unsafe working conditions. But the purpose of them all is the same: to preserve confidence in human association, to defend human dignity, to restore the balance demanded by commutative justice.

It is necessary to note here that the one who has suffered injustice is not for that reason permitted to be unjust in return. It is right to expect that the prankster who spray painted the front of my house be responsible for cleaning up the damage that has been done. It is not right to demand that the prankster repaint the whole house. In our times we have seen a whole tidal wave of damage suits in which the request for redress seems to outweigh the real injustices that have been done. One gets the impression sometimes that people are eager to suffer injustices for the sake of the overblown settlements that can be squeezed out of them. The goal of commutative justice is balance, not further injustice.

Similarly, doing injustice to someone who may not feel the injury is still injustice. Stealing a few grapes in the grocery store and taking an unauthorized coffee break at work may not be crimes that cry to heaven for vengeance, but they are violations of commutative justice nonetheless.

There are limits to commutative justice, however. Not

everything is for sale, and not everything can be priced by the simple agreement of buyer and seller. It is not right, for example, for someone to enter an otherwise valid contract to take part in pornographic movies. It is not right for an employer to get an employee to agree to less than a living wage simply because the employee has no other options. In both of these instances the greater good of human dignity is being violated, and no one has the right to sell or buy human dignity. Commutative justice must always be practiced in the context of the fundamental principles on which all justice is founded. We'll be seeing more about this in the next two chapters.

I seem to remember seeing somewhere a picture such as Norman Rockwell might have painted. It shows a woman in a butcher shop. There is a piece of meat on the scale, and the butcher is slyly pressing his thumb down on the scale on one side while the woman is slyly pressing her thumb up on the scale on the other. Each was practicing injustice. Just Christians know that all thumbs must be off the scale if the balance of true justice is to be maintained.

What acts of commutative justice do I engage in day by day?

Do I have some responsibility for seeing that injustice is not done to me? If so, why?

Do I get angry when I feel I have been treated unjustly? If so, why?

9

Distributive Justice: A Fair Share

Commutative justice has to do with the rights and duties of individuals in the context of specific voluntary encounters, generally encounters of purchase or contract. Distributive justice has to do with rights and duties in the context of the common welfare. It deals with the just distribution of the goods of creation that God meant us all to share. If we chose to call commutative justice the justice of particulars or of specific exchange, we would call distributive justice the justice of commonality or of general sharing.

We have already seen the foundations for distributive justice in our treatment of the general principles of all justice. God created the earth for us all. Our human dignity gives each of us a right to that portion of the earth's goods that we need to live a truly human life. We are jointly responsible for seeing to it that this right can be asserted in practice by all of our brothers and sisters, especially the poor, who do not have the resources to defend their rights for themselves.

Distributive justice is called for in each of the several communities in which we live. As human beings who share the community of the world, we all enjoy the basic human rights that constitute our share of the common goods of the world. They include such things as food, clothing, shelter, education, private property, and the like. We dealt with these in chapter 6.

As citizens of our national or local communities, we have claims in distributive justice to other things: the use of public streets and parks, access to public schools, protection from lawlessness, coverage in whatever pension or health programs are provided to all citizens. These things are owed to us in justice simply because we belong, because we are participants in the life of this particular country or city or town.

The family community is another context for distributive justice. Every family member has a right to his or her share of the goods that go with being a member: love and affection, housing, education, and the like.

The norm by which distributive justice is measured is different from the norm of commutative justice. We saw in the last chapter that the standard for commutative justice is strict numerical equality. I must pay exactly what I owe and get exactly what I paid for. The norm for distributive justice is not strict numerical equality but basic minimum need.

It is not the case that, as a member of the universal human family, I have a right to my precise fractional share of the world's wealth. I have a claim in justice to what I need to satisfy basic human needs, not more. Similarly, if I live in a town of five hundred people, it does not follow that I have a right to use the public park one five-hundredth of the time and that others have to keep out when I am using my share. Distributive justice is not a matter of equality but of minimum necessities and of general sharing.

It is not, therefore, unjust for some to be rich and others to be poor. This is a natural thing given the differences of human talent and luck, human energy, and appropriate human ambition. What is unjust is for some to have more than they need while others do not have enough for the basic needs of their human existence. Distributive injustice is not measured by numbers (as commutative injustice is) but by involuntary human misery or unfair exclusion. That society is unjust in which any member, through no fault of his or her own, cannot live a decent human life or does not have access to what is intended for everybody.

Given the demands of distributive justice, therefore, care for the poor in society is a matter not of voluntary charity or benevolence but of right. Everybody has a right to his or her share, and those who do not have their appropriate share have a claim on the others. The others, in turn, have an obligation to provide what is needed for the basic common good of all. Like commutative justice, distributive justice is a matter of real rights and real obligations.

But how is distributive justice exercised in practice? Obviously, it's not up to me personally to provide food and shelter for an uprooted victim of a war far away. It's not up to me personally to see that the streets are kept in repair so that everybody can use them. Distributive justice is the concern of society at large. In practice, this means that distributive justice is a concern of government.

When our national government provides for subsidized housing or food stamps or medical care for the indigent, it is attending to its responsibilities for distributive justice. The specifics of the various programs may vary from time to time. There may be appropriate differences of opinion about the best ways to see that the basic needs of everybody are taken care of. Some programs may be more efficient than others. Given human perversity, there will almost certainly be abuses in any program of social welfare. But the one thing that government cannot do is absolve itself of concern for the minimal needs of the governed. Such a posture amounts to legalized injustice. It constitutes social sinfulness.

When we look at the worldwide family of humanity, things get more complicated. It is clearly an injustice for people in one country to have literally more than they know what to do with, while people in other countries are starving to death. Over the centuries humankind has learned how to take care of the needs of family members or fellow tribesmen or the poor in villages and towns. We do better at the national level than we used to. But we have not yet learned how nations can take responsibility for the needs of their neighboring countries. This is because we have settled on the distinct, independent national state as the unit of government. As our world grows smaller, we are learning that such a unit is no longer adequate to deal with basic human claims for distributive justice. Programs of foreign aid are a step in the right direction, but they are obviously not an appropriate definitive solution. Gradually, richer countries are beginning to realize that their relationships with poorer countries cannot be based merely on economic self-interest. There are claims of justice to be satisfied, too.

So far we have been talking mostly about the individual's rights to a minimum fair share and of the community's obligation to provide that minimum fair share. But individual rights also involve individual obligations. Even as it is unjust for government to overlook the basic rights of its citizens, so also it is unjust for the individual to overlook his or her obligations for the well-being of all. The complexities of distributive justice may not be used as a cover for laziness. If I already enjoy the minimum I need, I nonetheless still have responsibilities for others. Some of these responsibilities I can exercise at a person-to-person level through private social agencies. Some I exercise by providing my fair share toward maintaining the government's responsibilities for distributive justice.

It's a lot easier to wiggle away from distributive justice than it is from commutative justice. In commutative justice both what I am supposed to get and what I am supposed to pay are clear. In distributive justice there is always a whole menu of questions. Why should I pay my taxes fairly when I know that the man next door cheats on his? Why should I worry about the other guy getting what's his when I already have what's mine? Are these costly social programs really effective? Why should our government be helping some foreign country when we have our own poor at home? Is everybody really sure that the money we send over there is used for what we send it for and not to line the pockets of corrupt politicians? Distributive justice is as messy as commutative justice is clear. For that reason, distributive justice is more difficult to practice than commutative justice is. But just Christians know that it is not for that reason any less real, any less urgent, any less demanding on our agenda in bringing forth justice.

In the last twenty-four hours, how have I exercised my rights to distributive justice?

In the last twenty-four hours, how have I fulfilled my obligations in distributive justice?

How just are the various communities in which I live?

10

Social Justice:
A Fair Say

We have seen that distributive justice is different from commutative justice, although both are concerned with rights and obligations: commutative justice generally involves individuals and exact numbers, while distributive justice has to do with communities and with basic needs and general sharing. In this chapter we will deal with another kind of justice: social justice.

The term *social justice* has been used in several ways in the Catholic tradition. Sometimes it is the equivalent of distributive justice. More recently, however, the term *social justice* has been used to designate the right and obligation of individual persons to be involved in determining the way in which larger social, economic, and political institutions of society are organized. The bishops of the United States used the term this way in their pastoral letter on economic justice in 1986 and went on to say that this form of justice can also be called "contributive" because it involves the duty of all who are able to do so to contribute to creating the structures that are necessary for the welfare of the whole community (see *Economic Justice for All,* no. 71). This is the sense in which I am using the term here.

The basic demand of social justice is that all those who are qualified have a voice in the establishment and the workings of the structures of distributive and commutative justice. Human beings have a right and an obligation to contribute to the society in which they live, and their contribution consists not merely in paying their share of the expenses but also in helping to determine how general rights and obligations are to be identified and distributed.

Social justice, as I am using the term here, is a relatively new aspect of the general demand of justice to give to each what is his or her due. In times past, there were those who ruled and those who obeyed. In its simplest form, justice in society was the concern of the king. The king alone was responsible for seeing that basic human needs were met and that private agreements and contracts were observed. The king alone was responsible for the system. This was an acceptable approach when very few people were educated and when most people had to spend most of their time and energy on the demands of survival.

But as humanity developed, it became clear that other people might have something to contribute also. As human society became more complex, it also became clear that no single individual had all the answers. The right to have something to say about the way things should be was first extended to small groups of advisers who served at the pleasure of the ruler. Then it became clear that participation in government was not the prerogative of the few but rather the privilege of all those who were affected by what government demanded and did. As our Declaration of Independence saw it, government is instituted to insure the rights of everyone and derives its just powers from the consent of the governed. Everybody has a right to be heard. Everybody should have his or her fair say.

This approach to justice in society is based in part on the principles that we have already discussed. Every human being has an inherent worth that does not depend on anything other than the individual's humanity. Every human being shares responsibility for the development of the world. Every human being is called to look out for others.

This having been said, however, it does not automatically follow that every human being should have a say in the structuring of distributive and commutative justice. One could argue that human dignity can be maintained and human responsibility exercised on the narrow scale of the individual even if broader concerns are taken care of exclusively by those who are more wise and more expert. One might contend that a kind of societal "Big Brother" is better equipped to look after more difficult matters.

The problem with such an approach, we have learned, is that it simply doesn't work and is ultimately unfair. Powers of governance that are not responsible to the governed almost always slide toward tyranny, a tyranny in which the wants of the ruler take precedence over the needs of the ruled. Moreover, the rule of one person or of a small group, to the exclusion of all others, suggests that the others have nothing to offer, no insight to promote greater justice. It deprives everybody but the select group of a portion of their human dignity, of the right to exercise human responsibility in a field wider than their particular network of relationships.

All this is not to say that everybody is qualified for every responsibility. Obviously, some women and men have greater talents in assessing the needs of society and in bringing forth justice for the community at large. Obviously, there are situations in which large numbers of the society's members are so oppressed by dehumanizing poverty and a lack of access to education that they are unable to take part in the general concerns of government. Social justice does not demand that everybody have equal voice and equal power in every context. Social justice does demand, however, that each society work toward that condition in which every member is capable of making his or her appropriate contribution to the well-being of all. A society that deliberately and permanently excludes people from participation in its business is an unjust society.

We have seen that commutative justice is generally quite clear. I have an obligation to pay for what I got and a right to get what I paid for. Distributive justice is more complex. The specifics of right and obligation cannot be determined in terms of strict mathematical equality. Social justice is still more complicated. How is the participation of the individual to be determined? If there are limits to participation, as is almost necessarily the case, what should these limits be? Is the form of government that is appropriate for a highly industrialized society in which most people have a significant level of education also required for a country in which most of the citizens are illiterate or inexperienced in any kind of society beyond their family or tribe?

But if social justice is complicated, it is not for that reason an impossible ideal. Our common humanity is still developing. We still have a lot to learn. But some things are clear.

One is that human beings have the potential to govern themselves, a potential that must be fostered and helped to grow as a matter of right. Every human being has the right to be heard, if not about all the specifics of legislation and policy, at least as regards his or her basic human needs. Every human being has the right to participate in governance to the extent that he or she is capable. Everybody has a right to a fair say.

Another thing that is clear is that there are also obligations in social justice. Apart from the obligation of those who govern to respect the rights of the governed, there are the individual obligations of private citizens. The most basic of these is the obligation to participate. We don't all have to run for public office or be members of a political party, but we have to accept our responsibility for what goes on in the society in which we live. If nothing else, this means voting conscientiously and letting those who represent us know that we expect them to be honest and just.

There is also the obligation to defend the social justice rights of others. No just person may allow others to be marginalized, pushed aside as unimportant, deprived of choice and voice. If our brothers and sisters are excluded from participation, it is up to us to see that such an injustice is not allowed to stand unchallenged.

To get a clearer picture of what is involved in social justice, let's imagine a country that is governed by a wise and kindly ruler. The ruler sees to it that there is food and housing and work and education for all his people. They don't have to worry about a thing. But the ruler alone makes all the decisions. He may be wise and kindly, but he is also unjust because he is disregarding the human responsibility and the human dignity of his people. He is depriving them of their basic right to participate in forming the world in which they live. In a country like that, just Christians would have to be revolutionaries.

How do I practice social justice?

What limits are there on my participation in determining the way our country is run? Are these limitations just?

Does anything need to be changed in the structures of our society? What? Why? How?

11

Justice and Charity: What's the Difference?

Some time ago a friend and I were talking about justice. He said, "You know, it seems that lots of things that we used to consider as charity are now looked on as justice. Helping the poor was considered an act of kindness, something we did out of the goodness of our hearts. Now it seems to be an ongoing obligation, a debt that we owe. Has something changed here?" I suspect that many people have asked that question. It is a good one and in answering it we can clarify our ideas about both charity and justice.

Charity, of course, has many meanings. It can mean our share in the life of God, a synonym for grace. It involves God's love for us and our response to that love. Charity can mean gentleness in word or action toward others. "She is filled with charity. No harsh word has ever passed her lips." Charity can also mean generosity toward those in need. "He is very active in works of charity." This is the sense in which I intend to deal with charity here.

Charity, in this sense, is a voluntary act of kindness that is done to help somebody else. When I throw some coins into the Salvation Army kettle at Christmas time, I am doing a work of charity. I am not responding to any specific claim. Nobody can force me to do what I do. There is no criterion to determine when I have given enough. I am giving out of the goodness of my heart to help others in some way or other. Charity is voluntary, open-ended, personally motivated, fundamentally affective. It is an act of graciousness that I do because I choose to do it. Granted, I may be motivated by love of God and love of my neighbor, but what and how I give are matters of my own personal determination.

Justice is different. This difference is easiest to see when we are dealing with commutative justice. When I perform an act of commutative justice, it is not up to me to decide whether to do it or not. Justice is a demand to which I am obliged to respond. Justice is also quantifiable in a way that charity is not. If I owe something to somebody, I owe what I owe and nothing more. When I have paid what I owe, the obligation has been fulfilled and I don't owe any more. Similarly, there is an impersonal quality about justice. It doesn't matter how I feel about myself or about the person to whom I owe something. I have an obligation to fulfill and that's all there is to it.

The difference between charity and justice is less clear when we are dealing with distributive and social justice. Every human being has certain basic rights, real rights to things like food, clothing, and shelter, rights to participate in determining the structures of the society in which he or she lives. This means that others have obligations, obligations to protect basic human rights for everybody, obligations to see to it that others get what is coming to them, obligations to promote the participation of everybody in the making of a just society. These rights and these obligations are less specifically determined and less clear than our rights and obligations in commutative justice, as we have already seen, but they are rights and obligations nonetheless. To see that people have what they need to live a decent human life and to play an appropriate role in society, therefore, is not a matter of charity but a matter of justice.

Yet in this realm of distributive and social justice there seems to be a kind of overlap of charity and justice, and it is this overlap that blurs the distinction between them and gives rise to the question we are discussing. The overlap arises from two causes.

On the one hand, our ideas of human rights have developed over the centuries of human history. Not too long ago it was taken for granted that poor people were poor because that was God's will for them. They had no right to anything more, and those who were better off were called to be kind to the poor, to help alleviate their misery, not because the poor had any claim in justice to an improvement of their lot, but because God took pity on them through the agency of those who had been given more. The standard response to human misery was charity, not justice.

Gradually it became clear that things didn't have to be this way. People began to realize that human institutions and human conditions were the result of human decisions and that these decisions could be changed. Human misery came to be seen as a manifestation not of God's will but of the imperfections of human society. Those who lived in misery were the victims of these imperfections and, as such, had the right to expect and demand that things be different. Human society began to be seen not as a changeless structure sent down from heaven but as a human construction that had to be bettered. If society could be changed for the better, then the rights and needs of everybody could be better cared for. And if society could be changed for the better, it had to be changed for the better. It became clear that charity was no longer enough.

We are living in a time when these ideals of distributive and social justice are still relatively new. (For example, when Pope Leo XIII taught in 1891 that an employer owes a living wage to those who are employed, he drew forth a chorus of scorn and disbelief.) Whereas in the past, justice was narrowly confined to the categories of commutative justice, we are now becoming aware that the realm of rights and obligations, of claims and duties is a far vaster field than we used to think. Justice is taking over areas that used to belong to charity, and the distinction between the two is not yet clear to many.

The second reason for the overlap of justice and charity is that, even when we are aware of human rights and obligations in distributive and social justice, we don't always know in detail how we are to respond. In every town and city there are people who live in misery, people who are willing to work but who can't find employment, and people oppressed by racial and economic prejudice. They do not enjoy the appropriate exercise of their human rights. They are marginalized and excluded. This is unjust, but the rest of us know that we cannot remedy their situation alone or immediately. Yet their needs are present and real. For that reason, we feel ourselves called to exercise works of charity. We get involved in providing food and clothing and housing, in private job training programs, in organizations dedicated to eradicating prejudice. These are works of charity because we do not have a specific obligation to do these specific things. Yet they are also works of justice because they constitute in some small and imperfect way a response to the obligation that we all share to promote distributive and social justice.

Something has indeed changed in our ideas about charity and justice, and that which has changed is the awareness of what we owe. Christians have always believed that they are called to love their neighbor, especially the neighbor who is poor. We owe our love to our neighbor. Now we are learning that love for our neighbor is not merely a matter of occasional acts of kindness offered because we feel so inclined but also a matter of long-term and demanding effort to help our neighbor become everything that God

meant him or her to be. Voluntary acts of charity are important in the life of the Christian believer, but they are no
longer enough to express fully the love we owe our neighbor. We are beginning to become more aware that we owe
our neighbor justice as well, a wider and deeper kind of
justice than the simple justice of fair exchange between
individuals.

Charity and justice are not the same thing, yet they are
related in ways that we may not always have seen before.
They are both manifestations of the love of God, a love that
we are all invited to receive and called to extend to the
world around us.

Just Christians are charitable Christians, but their charity is exercised not because of the abundance of what they
have or because of the generosity of their hearts, but
because of their awareness of what they owe.

*What acts of charity do I practice? Is there a dimension of justice
in them?*

Does justice necessarily involve kindness?

*Are there situations in which something more than justice is
called for?*

Conclusion: Portrait of a Just Christian

When I was working on my degree in classics at the University of Cincinnati, I did a study of classical portrait sculpture. I learned that, at certain periods, the portraits were very realistic, down to the smallest detail. At other periods, the portrait sculptures were more idealized. They were portrayals of individuals, to be sure, but seen in a rather general way, without all the minute particulars. In this chapter I offer a portrait of a just Christian, not a detailed portrait of a real individual but a sort of general portrait, yet one that might enable the viewer to distinguish the just Christian from other people. I have chosen to do the portrait of a man named Justin. The portrait of his sister, Justine, would include almost all the same elements.

Before all else, Justin is a Christian believer. He knows that the worth of his life lies not in success or wealth but in his relationship with the Lord Jesus, a relationship that was conferred on him in baptism and that he is called to develop and deepen throughout the course of his whole life. He knows that the implications of this relationship extend to every aspect of his existence and that there is never a time when he can say that he has done enough for the Lord and can now rest with the degree of closeness to God that he has reached.

Justin also knows that his relationship with the Lord Jesus must be expressed in his relationship with the people around him. It's not a private thing between him and the Lord.

People know that Justin is an honest man, a man of his word. He doesn't promise more than he knows he can deliver, and when he makes a commitment he keeps it. You never have to worry about whether Justin means what he says.

He a person who is careful about money. It's not that he is tightfisted but rather that he looks ahead and never allows his obligations to outrun his resources. He pays his bills on time. He doesn't buy what he can't afford. He makes it a point to read the small print on his credit card statement so that he knows exactly what is expected of him. He counts his change carefully when he buys something, not only to be sure that he has what is coming to him but also to be sure that the storekeeper hasn't shortchanged himself.

He expects other people to treat him fairly. If he feels that he has been cheated in a business transaction, he will make an issue of it. As he sees it, allowing others to be unjust is almost as bad as being unjust yourself. Yet he is not the type of person who will move heaven and earth to resolve some petty dispute. He may content himself with lodging a calm protest and then moving on to other things. He realizes that there has to be a sense of proportion in the pursuit of justice and that sometimes relinquishing the fine details of one's rights can be a form of charity.

Justin works hard for his employer. He knows that he owes a just day's work for a day's just wage. But he also works hard because he knows that his work makes a contribution to the development of the world and to the well-being of others in the society in which he lives.

Justin is not what you would call a political activist, but he is aware that he bears a measure of responsibility for what goes on in the world around him. For that reason, he makes it a point to inform himself of current social issues. He knows that not everything is as it should be in our society. He is concerned about employment opportunities and housing and education for everybody. He wonders whether our country is living up to its responsibilities to the rest of the world as well as to its own people.

He tries to understand what the various political and social leaders are proposing about these matters and judges the proposals according to his own awareness of human rights and of practical possibilities. He knows the names and addresses of his representatives in city hall, in the state capital, and in Washington, and he lets them hear from him with some regularity. "I may not always be right," he thinks. "I may not have all the answers. But at least they will know that somebody is watching. If nothing else, somebody has to keep asking the questions. Somebody has to keep saying that there is still more to be done."

Justin wouldn't dream of letting an election go by without voting. He looks on his right to vote as a responsibility more than as a privilege.

But Justin does not content himself with thinking about the issues and with reminding others that something has to be done about them. He is anxious to do what he can personally. He is an active member of his parish's St. Vincent de Paul conference, and he always participates in the parish's Christmas giving tree. He is enthusiastic about the American bishops' Campaign for Human Development not only because it enables those in need to better their situations but also because it educates the faithful at large about the demands of distributive and social justice.

Not many people know that Justin tithes. He gives ten percent of his gross income to his parish and to other charitable causes. He's not trying to bribe God by his generosity. It's more a matter of an awareness that the resources that he has carry with them an obligation to care for others. He looks on his tithe not as an act of charity but rather as a symbol of his willingness to pay up what he owes to the betterment of the world. He sees it as an act of justice.

Justin does not look on himself as some sort of specialist in justice. There are lots of other things in his life that occupy his interest. Yet he consciously strives to see that everybody has what is coming to them and that things become what they should be. He looks on this as part of his responsibility as a human person. It's an important aspect of being what God made him to be. For Justin, justice is a matter of consistency.

It seemed good to conclude these reflections with this portrait, general as it is, in order to give some idea of how the demands and complexities of justice can be lived out in practice. It is my hope that those who look at the portrait will not only be able to clarify their own ideas about justice but may also find something there to imitate, something to challenge their own exercise of justice.

In the final analysis, justice is not so much an obligation as a gift. It is a multifaceted opportunity to take part in God's loving care for the world, to assist God in making the world everything it was meant to be, to participate in the development of the deepest aspects of the humanity we share. When justice does not flourish, our human life together becomes impossible. Where there is real justice, our earthly existence is at its best.

It may be that there are two fundamental approaches through which God involves himself in the world. One is the enterprise of love: God's free decision to create us, to care for us, to bring us ever closer to himself. The other is the enterprise of justice: God's will to have us be everything that he had in mind for us, to have us develop all the potential that he put into us, to make us responsible for ourselves and for one another. Through God's gift, we are enabled to participate in these two enterprises of love and of justice. Neither can be divorced from the other. Justice is love in the context of rights. Love is justice in the context of personal concern. Love without justice is patronizing. Justice without love is spiritless and cold. Each is a facet of the godliness that we are called to share with our heavenly Father and with one another.

In the book of the prophet Micah (6:8), God tells us that what is expected of us is to act justly and love tenderly. In Matthew's gospel (1:19), when the evangelist wants to describe the loving and upright spouse of Mary, he says simply that Joseph was a just man. And in Isaiah (42:3), the servant whom God loves above all others responds to God's love by bringing forth justice. Just Christians are just because they are loving.

Is there anyone I admire for his or her practice of justice? Is this a loving person?

Which aspects of justice do I find most difficult to exercise in my life? Which are the easiest? Why?

Am I a just Christian?

Appendix 1: Just a Few Readings

*I*n the first chapter I mentioned that the Church has a whole body of teachings about justice. I chose not to cite that teaching in detail in the text because I did not want to make it too heavy, too technical. Yet there is merit in having some acquaintance with the sources. Some people might want to be reassured that what is offered in this book is really the Church's teaching. Others might want to pursue avenues of study and reflection that I chose not to travel in what I have written. So I offer a small selection of Church documents about justice, not the whole body of doctrine, to be sure, but a few examples, mostly recent, to give some idea of the depth and breadth of what the Church teaches.

The best place to start is that wonderful exposition of the Church's teaching, the *Catechism of the Catholic Church*. The catechism's most extensive treatment of justice is in numbers 2401 to 2463, where the catechism is treating the seventh commandment of the Decalogue, but there is also material on justice in number 1807 in connection with those human virtues that enable us to guide our conduct in accord with reason and faith. As is generally the case, the placement of the materials is itself instructive. Those who wish to follow up the catechism's teaching in greater detail will also want to refer to the numbers cited in the outer margins of the text.

The popes of the last hundred years have been great teachers about justice. In what follows I list some of the major papal documents about justice that have appeared in the last thirty years or so.

In *Populorum Progressio* (*The Development of Peoples*, 1967) Pope Paul VI deals with the structures of economic injustice, the limits of private property, and the distribution of the world's wealth.

Octogesima Adveniens (1971) marks the eightieth anniversary of Leo XIII's fundamental social justice encyclical on the economic aspects of labor, *Rerum Novarum*. In this apostolic letter Paul VI deals with contemporary social problems and highlights the role of individual Christians and local churches in responding to situations of injustice.

Paul VI's apostolic exhortation on evangelization in the modern world (*Evangelii Nuntiandi*, 1975) includes a section (nos. 29-39) that teaches that combating injustice constitutes an essential element of the Church's mission.

Justice and human work is the subject of Pope John Paul II's encyclical *Laborem Exercens* (1981). It develops and refines the Church's teaching on property and offers a critique of both capitalism and Marxism.

In *Sollicitudo Rei Socialis* (1987) John Paul II deals with the economic problems of the modern world and points out the duty of both nations and individuals to work for a just world society.

Centesimus Annus (1991) is John Paul II's encyclical to mark the hundredth anniversary of *Rerum Novarum*. Among other matters, the Pope deals with the significance of private property and the right of each human being to an appropriate share of the world's goods.

In *Evangelium Vitae* (1995) the pope writes about the most fundamental right of all, the right to life, and about the sources and implications of that right.

Pope John Paul II has spoken twice before the United Nations, and both times he spoke about justice. In 1979 he dealt with basic human rights and the threats to which these rights are subject. In 1995 he spoke about the need for international structures to guarantee justice in the relationships between nations.

Our American bishops as a group have taught about justice, too. It is a tradition that goes all the way back to 1919. Here are listed only three of the bishops' more significant recent teachings.

In 1983 the National Conference of Catholic Bishops issued an extensive pastoral letter entitled *The Challenge of Peace, God's Promise and Our Response*. This letter dealt with the justice and rights issues connected with war and self-defense.

In 1986 the bishops published another pastoral letter, *Economic Justice for All: Catholic Social Teaching and the U.S. Economy*. As its title indicates, this letter is primarily concerned with the justice issues inherent in the economic life of our own country. It speaks about human dignity, human rights, participation in the economic life of society, and the responsibility of society as a whole to enhance human dignity and protect human rights. It teaches that the pursuit of economic justice must be shaped by three questions: What does the economy do *for* people? What does it do *to* people? How do people *participate* in it?

Finally, in November 1995 the Administrative Committee of the bishops' conference issued a statement entitled *Political Responsibility*. This is one of a series of six such statements since 1976. These statements have been issued some months before presidential elections and list, in alphabetical order, the justice issues that need attention in our country. Their purpose is not to tell Catholics how to vote but to provide some orientation for them as they exercise their civic responsibilities in bringing forth justice.

This listing of Church documents gives some idea of the

Church's richness in teaching about justice. It also high-lights the complexity of the issues that involve justice. If nothing else, it suggests that bringing forth justice is not an easy task. Yet it is a task to which the Lord and his Church call us to be attentive and faithful.

Appendix 2:
A Catholic Framework
for Economic Life

*A*s followers of Jesus Christ and participants in a power-ful economy, Catholics in the United States are called to work for greater economic justice in the face of persistent poverty, growing income gaps, and increasing discussion of economic issues in the U.S. and around the world. We urge Catholics to use the following ethical framework for economic life as principles for reflection, criteria for judgement and directions for action. These principles are drawn directly from Catholic teaching on economic life:

1. The economy exists for the person, not the person for the economy.

2. All economic life should be shaped by moral principles. Economic choices and institutions must be judged by how they protect or undermine the life and dignity of the human person, support the family, and serve the common good.

3. A fundamental moral measure of any economy is how the poor and vulnerable are faring.

4. All people have a right to life and to secure the basic

necessities of life (e.g., food, clothing, shelter, education, health care, safe environment, economic security).

5. All people have the right to economic initiative, to productive work, to just wages and benefits, to decent working conditions as well as to organize and join unions or other associations.

6. All people, to the extent they are able, have a corresponding duty to work, a responsibility to provide for the needs of their families, and an obligation to contribute to the broader society.

7. In economic life, free markets have both clear advantages and limits; government has essential responsibilities and limitations; voluntary groups have irreplaceable roles, but cannot substitute for the proper working of the market and the just policies of the state.

8. Society has a moral obligation, including governmental action where necessary, to assure opportunity, meet basic human needs, and pursue justice in economic life.

9. Workers, owners, managers, stockholders and consumers are moral agents in economic life. By our choices, initiative, creativity and investment, we enhance or diminish economic opportunity, community life, and social justice.

10. The global economy has moral dimensions and human consequences. Decisions on investment, trade, aid and development should protect human life and promote human rights, especially for those most in need wherever they might live on this globe.

According to Pope John Paul II, the Catholic tradition calls for a "society of work, enterprise and participation" which "is not directed against the market, but demands that the market be appropriately controlled by the forces of society and by the state to assure that the basic needs of the whole society are satisfied." (*Centesimus Annus*, 35) All of economic life should recognize the fact that we are all God's children and members of one human family, called to exercise a clear priority for "the least among us."

The sources for this framework include the *Catechism of the Catholic Church*, recent papal encyclicals, the pastoral letter *Economic Justice for All*, and other statements of the U.S. Catholic Bishops. They reflect the Church's teaching on the dignity, rights and duties of the human person; the option for the poor; the common good; subsidiarity and solidarity.

©1997 by the United States Catholic Conference, Washington, D.C. This statement is available in poster and card format, both English and Spanish, from USCC Publishing Services (1-800-235-8722).